JOURNEY WRITTEN

JOURNEY WRITTEN
Faith. Obedience. Execution.

A Memoir by
BRIT LASHAE

Disclaimer: For privacy reasons, some names, locations, and dates may have been changed.

Copyright © 2020 by Brit Lashae

All rights reserved. No part of this publication may be reproduced, stored in a retrieval system, distributed, or transmitted in any form or by any means, including photocopying, recording, or other electric, or mechanical methods, without the prior written permission of the author, this also includes conveying via e-mail without permission in writing from the author.

Unless otherwise noted, all Scriptures quotations are taken from the CSB (in)courage Devotional Bible.
Copyright © 2018 by Holman Bible Publishers Nashville, Tennessee. All Rights Reserved.

Email requests: hello@britlashae.com

ISBN 13: 978-1-7367389-5-5

Printed in U.S.A

First Printing, 2020

2nd Printing, 2023

Published by Journey Written ®
Journey Written ® Book-Writing & Publishing
Visit our website at www.JourneyWritten.com

DEDICATION

I would like to dedicate this book to God. You provided me the strength and courage to push through when I didn't know how.

Thank you.

PROVERBS 10:22

"The Lord's blessing enriches, and He adds no painful effort to it."

Please Lord give me your wisdom and revelation for the day.

TABLE OF CONTENTS

Introduction V

Faith 1

Obedience 23

Execution 35

Meet the Author 63

INTRODUCTION

In this book, I will take you on the journey of how I got to know what my calling from God was. I will tell you about the journey to wholeness and my purpose, and how wholeness really helped me execute my calling. This journey was made up of a lot of tears, giving up, isolation, and low spirits. I started to have a hardened heart, but in the end, I learned obedience, I became whole, and learned how to fight. When I say fight, I mean fighting in the spirit and renewing my mind. Most importantly, I learned how to have a true relationship with God. Throughout this book, you will see that as my faith and healing transformed so did my business. You will see that as I got closer to wholeness, I was truly able to start birthing the things God called me to, and when I finally accepted that I was whole, I was able to walk in my calling with full authority.

I finally understood who and whose I was.

I felt worthy enough to do God's will and His way. I knew that even if I didn't have the "qualifications" that people thought I needed, I didn't need to prove qualified in their eyes, only my Father's eyes.

When I was broken, I couldn't see myself the way God saw me. Through my broken pieces, I didn't see my worth. I didn't think I was worthy.....

If you don't mind, I would like to walk you through my testimony of Faith, Obedience, & Execution.

GOD

provides me with *divine* direction, instruction, and strategy every single day. He has blessed me with wisdom.

FAITH

If you would have told me that I would be an Author, own multiple businesses, have a calling to bring God's women to wholeness, and also show them how to release their testimony, I would have not believed you. I would have laughed and honestly moved on.

I am an Actuarial Math Major, and I also have a MBA, so the thought of writing after college was a big no-no for me. In school, I dreaded anything related to writing. I always felt that a single paragraph was enough to explain what I was trying to say instead of the five-page paper the professor expected. I choose math because 2 +2 = 4 period, no going back and forth, the answer is what it says it is. That was my type of path, but I guess God had other plans for me. Plans that would challenge me to tell my story, plans that would allow me to use my creativity, plans that would bring honor to His Kingdom, plans that would lead His women to wholeness and release their stories.

To be honest, it's weird for me to even think about it.

One of the hardest things that I had to do during my journey was to accept that this is the woman that God has called me to be. I am not going to sit here and lie to you and tell you that this journey of truly finding my calling has been easy because it has not. I didn't think I was worthy of being God's vessel. Finding my calling and being obedient to it was tiring, and hard, and came with a lot of lessons. I almost gave up more than one hundred times, I didn't feel qualified… the list can go on endlessly. Many people think that it is easy to fully step into your calling with confidence and just do what God has called you to do, but it definitely takes levels of growth to get to this point, and then you have to maintain your confidence and relationship after that. I went through many character lessons, faith walks, endurance runs, wisdom seeking, spiritual warfare, and mind renewal journeys to get to where I am today. And no, they were not fun but I can agree that they were all much needed.

In 2017, God called me to heal. He told me that it was time to stop suppressing what was inside and that it was time to release, time to let go, time to be free, time to regain my power back. Everything that was inside me had to come out, everything that was holding me back, can't hold me back anymore.

Whew. The mere thought scared me! What was I going to do when I was free? What was I going to do with my power? I have never felt that way before. So wait, you're telling me that I have to "heal" from this pain that I have known basically my entire life? You are telling me it is "time to heal?"

These were the questions that I asked God when He told me it was time. The thoughts running through my mind of *"I can't do that," "I am used to feeling broken, wouldn't it feel weird to feel whole?"* I mean the thought of it sounds amazing, but scary at the same time. *I think I'm doing fine God....* I literally told God *"I am good"*, I think He has the wrong woman.

Then I felt Him. I felt His Holy Spirit encouraging me, I felt Him looking at me, and at that moment, He reminded me He's mine and I am His.

Being a survivor of sexual abuse, depression, anxiety, guilt, suicidal thoughts, low self-esteem, and shame – after 12 years I had finally made the decision to heal. I never really understood what it meant to heal. I didn't know there was a healing process. Growing up, I was known to be the one who accomplished everything, the one who always had a smile on her face, the one who uplifted others, but deep inside I always longed for the one who would make my day, who would be the one to uplift me. Was I really ready for this?

I have to be completely honest with you that even though God told my spirit that it was time to heal, I had to make the decision that I was ready to heal, and it was not an easy decision to make. I had to make up my mind that I was not going to be afraid to be free, that I was actually going to work on having power over my life, having a purpose in life, having a passion. I had to make a choice to allow God to birth "the me", I am talking about the "inner me," the me that is inside. I had to allow Him to do His work.

During my journey I have gained a better understanding of regaining my power, being intentional, and healing as a whole. Power means the ability to do something. Intention means on purpose. Healing means to make sound or whole. You put this all together and get "the ability to do something on purpose to make sound or whole." That is what I am continuously striving to be every day.

So as you can probably guess I said YES to God and at the time I didn't know that this was actually an act of "Obedience." After I said YES to Him, all I kept thinking about was: *Healing, Inner Healing, Healing the inside of you... What in the world does all of this mean?*

Not many people talk about this, I had the belief that I was a strong woman, as I smile on the outside and when I'm by myself, I cry, suppress, and carry on. I didn't know that when I decided to say Yes to God it would lead to other things in my life. I didn't know that saying YES to God about healing would take me on a rollercoaster ride of inner healing of my own, I just said Yes and kept it moving. I decided to SAY YES to God not realizing what the journey ahead of healing would be like. I didn't know when God called me to heal He would teach me vulnerability, He would teach me Self Worth, He would teach me how to have healthy relationships and friendships, He would teach me how to accept love and give it, He would teach me not to be so HARD all the time in order to protect myself, He would teach me grace over the hustle and grind, He would teach me rest, and most importantly He would teach me how to have a closer and stronger relationship with Him.

I said YES to God.

I promised Him that once I learned how to heal inwardly I would help other women with their inner healing journey.

THE JOURNEY OF BNPOWERED

"Mom I think I am going to start an inspirational Facebook page called BnPowered, it will be filled with quotes and encouragement to help and uplift others." I was so excited to start this journey, to begin the journey of BnPowered. I hurried to Facebook, created a business page and started inviting people to like the page. Every day I was dedicated to posting a quote to help uplift people, every day I was dedicated to helping someone else. On April 28th, 2017, I released the first video of my story. Something told me that it was time to start to release my *why*, the why behind why I started BnPowered. I was scared, I didn't know what my mom was going to think, I didn't know what social media was going to think, I didn't know what my coworkers were going to think, I just knew I had to do this for

God. I turned on my camera and I told a short version of my story. I opened up to the world that I was a overcomer of sexual abuse and major depression and that I wanted people on BnPowered to share their story, journey, and life unapologetically.

There were so many people that related to my story and related to what I have been through and who did not feel comfortable sharing but thanked me privately for my courage. This led me to do weekly BnPowered Tips where I would do a one minute inspirational video on my Instagram and Facebook page to help people start their week. I was so motivated that I started selling t-shirts. My first shirt was Beautifully Broken. I was doing vendor events. I was sharing my story through it and was proud of myself. This then led me to start a BnPowered Fitness group, because fitness was such a big part of my life as it helped me with depression and anxiety. I also wanted women to understand that they can look at fitness in a different way. I got my personal training license, started making workout plans for women, and doing all types of things.

Doing all of these activities, I realized that I was starting to revert back to not telling my story and not truly healing. I always called myself the queen of suppression, because I knew how to do it so well. I slowly started to turn the focus on inspiration only, not my story. I slowly started to move away from my story and be more of an encourager and motivator. The beautiful thing about this stage of my faith journey was that it came with a lesson, and it was able to birth something that would lead to my overall calling, my Armor of Words Book and Affirmation Cards.

ARMOR OF WORDS

It had been a little over a year since I started my weekly BnPowered Tips videos. I was going strong recording a 1 minute video every single week to inspire and uplift everyone. Then one day I sat down and thought to myself: "how can I repurpose this content, how can I reach more people with this mini inspiration?" All of a sudden, a book was downloaded into my spirit. I didn't know how to start a book, but I just started taking leaps of faith. I hired a virtual assistant to go through all of my videos and dictate my words into a document – I needed to see what this looked like on paper. After I received my document back, I used my gift of creativity and thought about how I could make the book different from any other and got straight to brainstorming.

Okay Brit, you love colors, you love uniqueness, you love short and to-the-point things, you love clean and luxury looks... and then it came to me: every page would be a different color, the fonts would be a mixture of regular and cursive, the colors would stand out, and the paper would be high end so that I could provide my readers with an experience while reading this book.

I really wanted people to feel special while reading Armor of Words. After I figured out the look of the book and how I wanted my readers to feel, I got my book designed, and started to go through the publishing process. I was so excited.

During my process of learning how to self-publish and finding a printing company that could print my book in high quality like I wanted it to, I went to an event in DC. I believe it was called friend speed dating. You go around and meet other young women in business and exchange information to learn more about their services and what they offer, and you exchange business cards. It was so much fun. I met so many amazing women who were just starting their business who were young, full of life, and loved to network. At the end of the event, there was a young woman, let's call her Abigail, who stated that she worked with upcoming authors to help them market their books and have a book launch, so of course I was curious. I went up to her and introduced myself, and she told me to email her the next day so that we can talk further.

I was thrilled.

I emailed her that night and told her more about myself and the book that I was releasing. This led to an experience I would never forget.

In our first meeting she told me that she promised God that she would serve first for 2 years before she took any payments from a woman. She said she would be happy to serve me, the only thing she asked was for a testimonial. *Wait, what!* This was a true blessing from God, because I didn't even know how I was going to pay her, but I just kept it cool and asked her what her prices were, but I definitely was not expecting that answer. She told me that we would be working together every single week until my book launch, and she would be helping me with every single detail because she believed in my book, and she loved that I was very serious about my follow up. She knew I was feeling guilty that she would be working with me for free. I am very big on respecting people's prices for their services but she assured me to not feel guilty of her serving, because God had her. So it began. We planned out the book launch, I was posting on social media for people to get their tickets, and then I got the first copy of Armor of Words.

The quality was amazing and I was excited.

I showed a few people the book out of excitement, and one person said: "That's it? People are paying for that? I mean it's nice, but it is only 36 pages and it looks like a pamphlet." Yup it happened, I started to have voices of doubt and negativity cloud my mind. I started to second guess everything I have worked so hard for, off of that one comment. I started to view my book differently, I started to think "*Am I going to embarrass myself by releasing this book?*", "*what if everyone thinks the same way as that person did?*" I cried that night because that one comment had me in doubt, had me in unbelief. I told Abigail about the comment, and right then and there she reminded me of who and whose I am, and that this book would touch the masses. Well thank God that He aligned me with another believer, because just like that I was back in the game. Nobody said a book has to be 1000 pages to touch a life, it's the words and the story that changes lives.

Encouragement: Doubt is contagious and if you are not careful you can catch it. It is so important to protect what God has put into your heart and spirit. It is so important to know and be confident in whose and who you are, because that one comment could have deterred me from birthing Armor of Words, that one comment could have delayed this blessing from God. Stand firm, surround yourself with people who believe in you, and know your truth.

On November 3, 2018, it happened. The launch was finally here! My family was in town, a few of my best friends were there, I had two vendors, my sorority sisters, coworkers, people I met, I even had a panel of amazing people that discussed how words and affirmations played a part of their life. Can I tell y'all that I cried while making my thank you speech – like thank you God for bringing me Abigail to help birth your vision, thank you for all of this love and support that I didn't even realize I had... just thank you.

Armor of Words Book sold out and to this day it is changing many lives.

BURNT OUT

Ending 2018 on such a high note, I was ready for the year of 2019. I went all the way in for my business, I hired a business coach, I was taking all types of classes, I had over 5000 followers on social media, I wrote my second book, and I was also doing my own inner healing at the same time. I was creating all types of digital products and courses, and about every other month I was doing free 5-10 day challenges for my audience. I was doing Instagram lives 2-3 times per week, weekly emails, sending out a weekly affirmation text, which costs money per user, and posting on social 3x a day all on my own. I was getting testimonials left and right from women who used my free stuff and how they were learning how to fully heal from the free resources. However, no one wanted to invest in the paid things with me as I was giving out so much free information and resources.

I mean why would they if I provided everything for free?

Yes, it is nice to serve, which is what I am good at doing but I was over serving. I was not honoring my boundaries. I had no boundaries in 2019, for myself or anything. I didn't honor rest, I didn't give myself the time I needed to truly practice self-care, I honestly thought burning myself out was honoring God, I thought that choosing my calling over anything else was honoring Him. I went into debt. I had a false belief that serving for the kingdom meant that it was a bad thing to make money for my business. I felt bad for asking for a sale without serving first, which led to true burnout. I started to get frustrated from doing everything for free, while I had to pay for everything on the backend. I noticed that I started to follow the trends of how others were utilizing their social media, and how people said they made 1k in 1 day, and I wanted that, I wanted that success, I was sick of being broke while helping others, and that led me into disobedience, which at the time I knew nothing about. I started to do things in my own strength, and create all types of products that were out of alignment with what God had planned for me. I started to hear more voices that were not God's own, and more false beliefs and negative self-talk erupted within me. Mental exhaustion quickly came, irritation built up while I was serving, and slowly a hardened heart began to surface.

Little did anyone know, I wanted to quit, and not do this anymore.

A few things about me:

I do not like a lot of attention but I didn't realize God was teaching me discernment and how to allow others in while still protecting myself.

I do not like a lot of people watching me and seeing what I am doing because I feel like people start preying on me and speak words of doubt and fear over my life. I didn't understand God was continuously teaching me how to be vulnerable but at the same time how to speak truth and positivity into my own life and cancel out anything that is not of Him.

I started to feel like the whole world was watching me, but I didn't know God was preparing me for my next level.

The pressures and the burnout that came with serving others and pouring into women when I was still healing myself were definitely something serious.

One day in the fall of 2019, I cried as I was sitting at my computer desk. It was too much to keep serving while I was still healing. My bank account was basically depleted, my credit cards maxed out, and I was trying to take care of myself. Now, I take things seriously when I say I am going to do something, and you know I promised God that I would heal and that I would help, but I couldn't serve with this spirit in me. I could not serve with a broken spirit like God needed me to, but I knew His women needed me, so I just cried in surrender, because I didn't want to break my promise to God or His women. That same day, after my ugly cry (we all know the ugly cry), I released everything to Him.

God then spoke to me and said: "I need you to make a Triggers resource and freebie for my women".

I was like: *What is a triggers resource, what does that even mean?*

He led me to Canva, and I created the resource in about 30 minutes. I created a landing page and posted it on social media, and literally within the first few hours it had over 100 downloads, and I received a testimonial within the next day.

"Thank you so much for the Triggers exercise because it made me realize a lot about me not wanting to be lonely. Identifying where the core of the issue laid, it helps me to start to really do some self reflections and know that "I am ok"! I have been really struggling with healing and coming to peace with being alone and being happy with myself, until I received your affirmations! They really help me on days when I just question why I am feeling this way? And they just give me life and push on a good day! Thank you so much!" ~ Melody

After the free resource was created, I created a free 10-day Triggered Challenge and had over 250 women join the challenge. The challenge impacted so many lives.

I was then led to create the Triggered Book & Workbook.

Wait! God, you want me to write another book, but a workbook this time?

I sat on my bed and looked up at God. It was something about books and workbooks that God was trying to tell me, but I just couldn't figure it out. I questioned: *What am I supposed to be doing with this, I don't understand why you have me creating this workbook, and I don't understand why you trust me to give this to your women, but for some reason I know you called me to write this and create this for a reason, so I have faith in you, God.*

I was back to feeling His peace like I used to feel at the start of this journey. There was no confusion, anxiousness, or worry that came with writing the Triggered Book & Workbook and the free resource. It all flowed so easily. You see how God led me right back to Books & Workbooks and Inner Healing. I was over here creating courses (He didn't tell me to do that), doing all these free challenges (He didn't tell me to that), taking all of these courses (He didn't tell me to do that), hiring coaches (He didn't tell me to do that), and doing entirely too much on social media (He didn't tell me to do that). Even though I derailed a bit and did things in my own spirit, He still led me right back into what I was called to do: be this Author He called me to be, be this creator of things involving Inner Healing and Wholeness, but y'all I still didn't fully accept this. At the time, I didn't realize that I would never reach the fullness of who God called me to be until I accepted this piece of my life.

Going through this season was not fun, to say the least. I learned how to break my silence. It taught me about discernment and disobedience so that I would understand what disobedience looked like. No one ever taught me what disobedience looked like or what it exactly meant in regards to following God, all I knew was to *hustle hustle hustle*, like everyone else, not realizing that there was another way to do things. I had to go through this season of disobedience in 2019 in order to understand what obedience means, to understand the difference of His strength versus my strength, and the difference of working in peace and grace versus confusion. I realized when I just trusted God everything worked out, but when I worried or allowed confusion in everything was all over the place, and I got off track. I also learned that unbelief will lead you into disobedience. Not believing that God will order your steps and that things will work out together for your good. This had me walking in my own spirit and getting off track because I didn't fully believe that I could do the work that He had set me out to do.

A faith-building season for me.

I had to start talking to myself in a different light and say: "Brit, stop running away from what God has called you to do and trust the process because when you run away you are doing everything that he has not called you to do." I learned that I found every opportunity to start creating projects and everything that was not assigned to me from Him, and that had to stop in 2019.

TESTIMONIALS FROM ARMOR OF WORDS BOOK

"I love the Armor of Words Book and affirmation cards! I have decreased my anxiety by reading my affirmations throughout the day and starting my day with a workout. I have already recommended this to many friends. My favorite affirmation was about giving thanks and being grateful because sometimes I forget to count my blessings and to focus on what I already have." ~ Deronda S.

"I bought them Armor of Words Book and Affirmation Cards as an Easter gift for my daughters. I loved the entire concept. I do believe words are power. This is another resource in the arsenal of positive thinking returns positive results." ~ Mary K.

"I LOVE the Armor of Words book and cards. They provide daily reminders to love yourself and be positive. When you start your day with such inspiration it helps make routine stressors a lot easier to handle. The mini workouts are an added bonus and have become part of my morning ritual before work. I would absolutely recommend this to a friend! I can't pick one affirmation that I love because they're all great!" ~ Amanda S.

"SOULFUL WORDS AND YES I WILL RECOMMEND ARMOR OF WORKS!!! My Favorite Affirmations in the book are JOY AND LOVE" ~ JACAYNLENE M.

"Armor of Words book has given me a different mindset in how I go about my day. It provides a positive light that was needed in my life to affirm how I want to move forward in 2018. I would definitely recommend it to a friend. "Have Faith in You"...affirms the reasoning on how others can have faith in me if I don't have faith in myself...self-awareness." ~ CC

TESTIMONIALS FROM TRIGGERED BOOK & WORKBOOK

"This is really good stuff. I never really thought alot about triggers but I definitely have some stemming from my mom and I's relationship. It's being told what to do. I didn't realize it until I moved out and spent the night recently and she told me something to do relating to my daughter and I reacted with a quick response but I felt the anxiety in my body too and knew it triggered me. It was good to recognize that. Now I'll be able to deal better. Thank you for Triggered." ~ Terri S.

"It's only Day 2 for Triggered and already feeling like I'm the woman for the job. Going all in. It's healing time!!! Hurt, afraid, terrified, uncertain, feeling like I got it and in the same breath wanna stop...But I can't. I won't. I am the dang woman for the job!" ~ Chokol

"Thank you so much for the Triggered Challenge, during the Past ten days the information I have received has been real and truly amazing open my eyes to so many questions, especially about myself. I am so thankful for your emails, every morning I looked forward for my triggered challenge, and even though the 10 days are over I will still continue to read over the challenge to better myself." ~ Tandy

"Brit! I really did enjoy this challenge! I always knew I had triggers but for some reason my emotions always got the best of me. This challenge really had me mad at myself instead of others. I finally had to hold myself accountable of the things said/done throughout my life. I now see I always have a choice. I hold my power, no one else can make me do or say anything. I highly recommend this challenge to my besties and love ones, who are on a journey to find themselves. I surely needed it after suffering a miscarriage last year. I completely lost myself, everyday is a challenge but with God's love and my families love I know Ill be back to myself. Thank you again Brit for this challenge, I hope you have a great Weekend." ~ T.

GOD'S
work speaks for itself,
everything *divinely* flows.
I rest securely.

OBEDIENCE

Journal Entry: God, please equip me, train me, and give me a strategy on what I am called to do. God, help me to follow your divine blueprint. Help me to not waver from your plan and will over my life.

This is the prayer that I went into 2020 with because I could not afford to have another year like 2019. My motto was Pray, Trust, Obey. Period. I didn't want to deviate from this at all, all I wanted to do was get back into my relationship with God and live life because the way I handled 2019 was not it. The way I did things my own way was not the way to go, and I learned a very important lesson, obedience vs disobedience.

JANUARY 2020

I started my podcast "The Brit Lashae Speaks Podcast," in January 2020. I needed a new way to tell my story and help my audience. I had to figure something out because I was still feeling the overflow of burnout from 2019, and it was bad. I knew that God had put into my spirit to start a podcast, so I stepped out on faith and did just that, but something still was not right within me. I didn't realize at the time that I was angry, disappointed, and had hardened my heart to my entire purpose because I put so much energy and faith in 2019, that I didn't even want to do this anymore, I didn't even want to give it my all at all. I was afraid to get burnt out or disappoint Him. I was afraid to make any decisions on my own anymore. I was still very sad and defeated about my finances. But, I thought about the promise I made to God in 2017, and told myself: "Brit, this year you are doing things differently, you are actually allowing God in to order your steps, you are actually allowing Him to be involved and be the CEO of the business, trust Him and see how this year goes."

I picked myself back up and kept it pushing.

I started to be intentional about studying my word and actually writing down Bible verses that I needed to make it through and study their deeper meaning. I promised God that I would journal to Him on a regular basis and have business meetings with Him. I promised Him that I would tithe every week no matter the cost. All I asked was that He divinely order all of my steps, refill my spirit, and renew my mind. I needed my spark back, I needed my creativity back, I needed my serving spirit back, I needed the happy believing in herself Brit back, so that I could deliver the promise I gave to God January 2017. I didn't want to give up, but at the same time I didn't know how I was going to keep going, I just had to have the faith.

January, February, March: I did the podcast, I posted on social media, I still had my email list going, I was journaling every day. I was tithing, I was doing everything that I said I was going to do but I was mentally exhausted. I was tired, I couldn't think anymore, I couldn't pour out the way I used to anymore. I wanted to be done with just everything, but I couldn't give up now. So, I started to do more research on what mentally exhausted meant. *Why couldn't I think anymore? Why did I feel burnt out again? Why didn't I want to speak to anyone on the phone because that would use brainpower? Why Why Why?*

Many times I would just sit in my car and do nothing. I would sit there and just cry not knowing what else to do to make sure that I fulfill my promise to God. I was tired, mentally, emotionally, physically, and spiritually. I didn't have anyone to talk to that would understand where I was coming from. Everyone I tried to talk to always said: "Well stop putting so much work into it," they didn't understand the type of work I was doing. I was alone.

ALIGNED FRIENDSHIPS

1/21/20 Journal Entry: Lord please send divine healthy relationships that are supportive in my life, in the name of Jesus, Amen!

Who would have known that by taking the chance to go to a Pitch Competition in 2018 would lead to such an amazing and God-ordained friendship and sister in 2020. I, for one, didn't. It was fall of 2018, and I was invited to a pitching workshop. Abigail was speaking, so of course I was going to go to support her. I went in and told her that I would take pictures of her as she spoke to put up on her social media. I looked around and scooped the room to see where I could get the best shots and where I could get a good seat to see everything. I sat down and introduced myself to the young lady who was sitting next to me, she was about 5 years younger than me. She introduced herself very confidently, so we spoke and exchanged information as we networked together. I told her how I was still fairly new to the area and she said we should definitely link up some time. She explained how she left her corporate job to start her own marketing business and I explained to her how I just finished writing my book and how I was preparing for a book launch with the young lady who invited me to this pitch competition.

Now don't get me wrong, I did not know that this was going to be a pitch competition. I thought it was going to be something where we learned how to pitch. Well, that was true at the beginning. In the end, we each had to take what we learned and apply it to real life. They brought in three investors who we had to pitch to and someone was going home with a cash prize. *Wait, I was not prepared for this. I do not know how to pitch, what is this, I think I will pass* – is what went through my mind. Well that wasn't quite the case, I did end up pitching. I didn't win but I met some pretty amazing women that day who would, in the near future, be exactly who God needed to be in my life in His divine timing.

I kept in touch with the young woman, who I met at the event – we'll call her Lesha. We started to go to happy hours together every other month, I would check in to see how she was doing. I began building a friendship with her; I didn't know anyone who lived close to me in Maryland as all of my friends lived closer to DC. I also wanted to start to build a network of other women who were in business.

Fast forward to 2020. I texted Lesha as I hadn't heard from her in a few months and we set up a happy hour to catch up. She said that she really needed some girl time and I was like *same sis*. I was excited to go to happy hour. I got dressed, and then I received a text from her that stated: "Brit there has just been a stay-at-home order issued by the governor and all restaurants have to shut down by 5pm today due to Covid-19." *Noooooo* is all I thought. I needed this, I had already been working from home for 2 weeks and I needed to get out and do something. *Dang Coronavirus, you just shut everything down!* I couldn't even go home to see my family, because they were also giving tickets to people who were disrespecting the quarantine and you couldn't travel out of state. *Oh Lord what am I going to do.*

Lesha and I decided to just do a phone call to catch up, and when I tell y'all that we were in the *same exact boat* regarding our spirituality within our businesses that God had blessed us with, in regards to complete burn out, and in regards to truly learning how to lean into Him to order our steps. It was like God matched us up specifically for a time like this. We will get back to this later in the book.

GOD CALLS THE UNQUALIFIED

Journal Entry 3/11/20: Hi God, I am angry. I am upset. I am disappointed and I FEEL DEFEATED. I don't know what to do with my life anymore. I have cried out to you. I have tried to see you but I can't find you. What am I doing wrong? In the name of Jesus.

This is the type of relationship God and I had built: where I could just come to him and tell Him how I really felt so that I could release it to Him instead of others. March 11th, 2020 is the day I found out I had to let go of the name BnPowered. God had other plans for me, but I didn't know what that was. I was devastated and angry. I sat on my bed with tears running down my face feeling all types of defeat, feeling like I let myself down, but most importantly God down.

How did I miss the mark?

I looked up at my wall and I saw the words Journey Written hanging up. I remember I wrote this name down in 2018 but I wasn't quite sure what God needed me to do with it, so I just wrote it down and put it on my wall like I do with everything He downloads in my spirit. There was something about the name Journey Written that wouldn't leave my spirit, so I walked up to the paper and just stared at it. I wrote: "book writing and publishing" on the paper. I realized that that was something to do with me helping women release their stories, but I knew dang well God did not call me to this, let alone start a book writing and publishing company. *What does all of this mean God? Oh, and how am I going to tell everyone that BnPowered is no more? Aren't they going to think that I am a failure?*

Was the "book writing and publishing company" my voice or was this God's voice?

I was trying to make every excuse not to believe that this is what He wanted me to do. I was trying to make every excuse to not be the author He wanted me to be, like *God this is not my thing.* I went back to crying, the voices in my head started taking over. There were so many thoughts running through my head of why He wanted to change directions, that I was not qualified for this type of work. *God, why would you choose me?*

I remained in unbelief for a few weeks, with the constant reminder of Journey Written on my wall. I never took it down, I just kept asking God to help my unbelief. At the time I didn't know that unbelief leads you off track. I started thinking I could start online courses, but it wasn't sitting in my spirit right. I started to brainstorm different t-shirt ideas, but that wasn't sitting in my spirit right either. Everything started to become difficult and cause confusion in my mind. And you know why? Because I wasn't supposed to be doing that! The only thing I was supposed to be doing was walking in faith of this Journey Written path that I had on my bedroom wall and being an Author that focuses on Inner Healing and Wholeness. I started to get angry again because nothing was working out right, nothing was coming to me with peace and ease, I still wasn't ready to accept all of this in my life.

On March 29th, I woke up with a lot of anxiety. I went into my prayer closet and just sat there, tears started to roll down my face – there was no stopping them. I journaled to God to give Him my worries, but these worries would not go away. I decided to get up and go to my desk to work on this online course that I started to create, but then I got this big headache and I couldn't focus. I turned on a sermon to try to refocus my mind, but that didn't help, I tried worship music: that didn't help. Nothing was helping me focus and do the work that I thought I was supposed to be doing.

Something is not right. Maybe I just need to get out of the house.

At that time it had been 2 weeks since I was quarantined due to Covid-19, and everything was closed. I walked to my car and just broke down. I couldn't take it anymore. I yelled to God as loud as I could: "God I am frustrated, I don't know what you need me to do, I have been trying and trying and trying and I get nowhere... WHAT IS IT?" When I released my frustration and anger, I felt this peace overcome me. I guess I needed a good scream. I just needed to open my mouth and make it known.

All I heard was: *It's time for Journey Written.*

ALIGNMENT AND AGREEMENT

On March 29th 2020, I learned again about God's peace. It surpasses all understanding. This was another test of learning the difference between walking in my own spirit versus God's spirit. A reminder to self, if it wasn't peace it wasn't God, if it came with confusion it wasn't God. I started to teach myself my own spirit's ways, so that I could be cautious of that, and to pause when it started to get out of hand. I got out of my car and walked back to my condo wiping my tears from my eyes so that my neighbors wouldn't see, but they probably heard my yell, so at this point, it didn't even matter. I had finally received God's peace. I fought it for a while even though I knew what He needed from me, but the key was that I was finally in alignment with what He had called me to do.

Once I got back in the house, I went straight to my journal so that I could write to God about everything that just happened and thank Him for His patience with me.

I also asked Him: *How do I start this as I have no knowledge of even how to begin this Journey.*

I walked out of my prayer closet and went into my living room. Lying on my floor was a flyer from this podcast event I went to before quarantine and it read Book Outline. I didn't know what this meant but I trusted that this was my answer on how to get started with Journey Written.

3/30/2020 Journal entry: God I am happy that you have provided me my purpose. Listen, you shut stuff all the way down. I was like, okay Father, you better shut operations down so that I can open the business you need me to open. Yes God, I accept the calling of owning a Book Writing & publishing Company YOUR WAY! TRUST ME LESSON LEARNED TO DO THINGS YOUR WAY! Let's Go God! I love you, in the name of Jesus, Amen, Brit

I finally accepted the calling. I was finally in agreement with God and Journey Written.

What a rollercoaster ride!

GOD
supplies all *creativity* and next steps.
I put my works with my faith.

EXECUTION

THE DEEP WORK

IT WAS TIME TO GET TO WORK. IT WAS TIME TO BE IN FULL OBEDIENCE and do what God had called me to do. It was time to execute. I couldn't go home to my family because only "essential employees" were allowed to be on the highway. I couldn't go visit my friends because I wanted to make sure everyone was safe, so it was literally the perfect time for me to focus and really dive deep into this thing.

There were three things that I felt I had to do as I dove into Journey Written: repent, get off of social media, and become whole. I wrote in my journal everything that I wanted to repent from and everything that I wanted to turn away from and then I read Psalm 51 every single day. Throughout my day I would repeat: "God create a clean heart for me and renew a steadfast spirit within me," from Psalm 51:10. This is what I needed Him to fill me up with, I couldn't do this on my own or with the same mindset and spirit that I had in the past. As God was doing the inner work within me I started to feel like I should get off social media. I honestly didn't know what that was about. I reflected on this thought and decided to take the leap and get off for as long as I needed to.

But what about my followers, what about my brand, everyone always says to show up for your audience every single day, to be consistent, but I knew I needed to do this and just completely log off, so that is what I did. I thought people would think that I was a failure, especially due to the way I left, but my focus was on being obedient.

I turned off all of my notifications on social media. It was time to do the deep work that only God and I could do together without all of the distractions. It was a learning season for me to not be influenced by all of the social media noise anymore. God didn't need me to compare myself to anyone else. He didn't need me looking at so and so and how they were healing or building their business. He needed me to focus on my relationship with Him. He needed me to be stronger in who I was and not who I thought I should be. He needed me to not be distracted as He was ordering my steps. The less distracted I was, the more clear I could hear His Holy Spirit as I had more time to focus on refilling my spirit. He needed God and Brit to spend intentional quality time so that I could heal and become whole.

I thought I was done after this but I just knew there were just a few more pieces that I needed to fully heal from in order to reach my wholeness.

Okay I repented, I got off of social media, so now what else do I need to be doing?

I decided to just sit still. I didn't know what my next move was supposed to be and I knew that I did not want to move in my own strength, as that is what made me burnout last year. Slowly but surely, I was led to my own Triggered Book & Workbook. Something was telling me that I needed to see what the last few of my triggers were to completely become whole. So I grabbed the book off of my shelf and started working on it again and some things were revealed to me that I had to face head-on and learn how to navigate. Little did I know this was the last step I needed to complete to become whole. My next level depended on this.

During my time off doing the last bit of deep work, God let me know that I had been doing all of the inner work this whole time, even though I may have been out of sync in 2019 with how I was operating and running the business. I still never gave up on my inner healing during that entire time. I still was putting in the necessary work and also bringing women along with me. To be honest, internally I felt like I gave up, but in reality, I never gave up hope. Truthfully, I never gave up faith, all I really was doing was building up my endurance and learning lessons of character development. I never stopped no matter how hard it got.

THE PILOT

Getting off social media, working through my triggers, and growing a closer relationship with God made me feel a bit isolated. I knew that no one in my life would understand the process that I was going through, so I literally had no one to talk to. It's not that the people that I have in my life don't care, it's just that they wouldn't understand why I had to do the things I had to do during this season of my life, and if I talked to them I would be filled with fear, doubt, unbelief, and I couldn't take that risk. This was my true definition of moving in silence with God. Only Him and I knew what was going on behind closed doors and I think that is exactly how He wanted it to be. I just had to learn how to embrace it and ask for his comfort. After all, God always knows what he is doing.

Now in the past, if God gave me an idea I would just run with it and be like *okay here we are what is next*, but this time was different. This time I felt that I needed to continue to move in silence. On April 7, 2020 I got out my pen and paper and wrote down Journey Written at the top. All I knew was that it was a Book-Writing and publishing Company. I didn't know how to start, what to do, I didn't even know what the heck Book-

Writing meant. All I knew is that I needed to start. I sat on my couch and started to cry, I felt stuck, I felt stagnant because I didn't know how to start or what strategy to undertake.

I knew nothing.

My aligned sister in Christ, the one I met at the Pitch Competition, Lesha, texted me at that specific moment and said: "Hey sis, what you up to?"

I replied: "crying."

She asked me why, and I explained to her everything I was trying to do. I knew if anyone would understand, she would, because she was the person who I talked to God about. She was the one who understood this process of allowing God to order your steps in His business. She owns a Marketing Company, so she texted me: "Sis I will help you come up with a strategy." I asked her the price for her services and she stated: "I will do it for free for you, I'm here to help push your purpose out."

Oh shoot! God did it again. He provided me with the help I needed in His divine timing.

On April 10, we had our first strategy session. I also asked her what she needed me to help her with because, since it was free, I didn't want to feel like I was taking advantage of anyone. She said: "Right now, we're focused on your vessel and fueling it." This help was definitely unreal. It confirmed that this was divinely ordered. My sister pulled out of me things that I didn't even know I had the answers to. I was blessed. After our session, I decided to start off with a pilot program so that I could test out what my company was supposed to look like. I made a waitlist, but I still wasn't on social media so I didn't know how people were going to know about Journey Written and our Pilot.

On April 21st, I decided to announce it on my podcast. I told my audience that I had a waitlist for a Pilot program and that this would be the perfect program if they wanted to write their story in a book. On April 24th, I had three ladies on the waitlist. One was from the podcast, and two from Instagram. I never officially announced anything on social media or had I been on social media, but my website had the waitlist link on it. I remember getting messages from the women and one of them stating that she had seen someone tag me in a post about being an author and she decided to check out my page and website. The two other women were stating that they had always wanted to work with me but didn't know in what capacity and that this was the perfect season in their life for me to work with them.

Wow, okay this was really happening.

I started to write out a group coaching program that I would open up to women to join and we would work together on their book for six weeks. I would tell them the ends and out of releasing their story and self-publishing.

Well, On April 26th, God gave me confirmation that I was supposed to start with one-on-one coaching and not group business together exactly how God wanted it to be. I was getting God's full business plan for Journey Written one step at a time. It felt good to be impacting lives, to help women release their story, to help them be encouraged to help another woman with what they have been able to overcome, but I was starting to feel burnt out again. I was once again pouring, pouring, pouring but not filling myself back up. It was quarantine so I wasn't physically in my church home, I didn't have my family near me, and I had to ask God how I could be a good vessel for Him while making sure I rested and took care of myself.

In asking God how I could be a good vessel for Him, God taught me boundaries and how to properly serve His Kingdom during the pilot program for someone like me who only knew how to serve but not receive. He led me to work on my clients' books on Saturday and Tuesday mornings so that I would have a dedicated schedule for just their books. He helped me break down the false beliefs of I have to only be a giver, of its bad to have wealth, of hustle and He moved me into grace, into receiving, into rest. and obedience.

I was finally getting the hang of things.

MY BABY BAG

7/11/20 is a day that I will never forget. Something was telling me to welcome wholeness into my life. For some reason, I just got this feeling over me that I was whole. But what did being whole really mean to me? I started to ponder this question more and more as I journaled. I wrote that I was going to start walking in the authority of my wholeness. For the majority of my life, all I knew was the broken Brit. This was a different version of me, my mind was renewed, I knew how to respond to situations instead of react, I put in the work in therapy, I put in the work on myself, and wholeness was finally here to welcome me in. I truly believe that wholeness means something different for each of us. For me, it meant that all of my broken pieces were completely healed, it meant that now I knew my triggers and how to maintain them, that when different situations came up in my life I had my tools in place on how to handle them. It meant that I would have to continue to push through and do the daily work to maintain my wholeness, it meant that I would have to learn this new version of myself.

Accepting my wholeness allowed me to accept the worthiness of my calling. I realized that I couldn't fully believe in myself and execute my calling until I understood that I was worthy enough to do this type of work that I didn't even think I was qualified for in the first place. In the corporate world, I was confident Brit, I knew my stuff, and there was education for days coaching. I had three women on the waitlist, I needed a price, I needed next steps. *What do I do?* I started to get sad because I felt like I couldn't hear God on the next steps, and I know you are probably thinking *Brit He has been providing you all these steps*, well it is not as easy as it sounds when you are trying not to move in your own spirit and hear God's voice over yours. To be honest, I started to be scared to move because I didn't want to lean on my own understanding. *Been there done that.* I spoke to Lesha and she told me that God would continue to order my steps as I made the next move.

Encouragement: One thing I want to encourage you all to do is to pray for discernment to hear God's voice because sometimes he will tell you to rest, to move, to be still, and it's important to know the difference. As you pray for this you will start to be put through mini-tests that will allow you to start to understand His voice and ways over your own and the enemy's. For me personally, when it is peace and no confusion at all, I know it is God's way. When I feel even a bit of anxiety, fear, or doubt, I know I am starting to get in my own way, and I have to teach myself to restart in order to get my peace back so that I can be led with grace and ease. This was definitely a season of learning what it truly meant to walk in alignment and agreement with the Holy Spirit.

Back in 2019, God gave me the price $497 to put on my Journey Written piece of paper. This price popped back up as I was thinking about how to even start this pilot program. I reached for my phone and called my sis, I said: "Hey girl, God only gave me one price, $497, it keeps popping up in my head." She said: "Well let's just try $497, and see what happens."

Have you ever seen that meme where the girl jumps off the cliff? Well, that is how I was feeling at that moment: like I was jumping off a cliff in faith. I grabbed my computer and started to draft up an email to invite the three women to join the pilot program and that it would be $497 for 6 weeks, and if they were interested I would love for them to book a call to learn more. On May 2nd I sent out the email, and 2 women automatically booked their call. On May 8th I had my first client, on May 13th, I had my second. No marketing of the pilot program, no big announcements. I only mentioned it on the podcast and added a link to my website, and in less than a month I had my first two clients. All I could do was give glory to the Most High.

I still didn't know what to do. I didn't know how the first meeting was going to go with these women, the plan, the outline... nothing. I went with the flow with my faith and works. That's all I knew how to do at this point.

On the day of each meeting with my ladies, I would get up early, do my usual praying and journaling, but then I would go to my business meeting journal and just sit and ask the Holy Spirit what He needed me to pour into my woman that day – what was the strategy and blueprint for this day, and each and every time He would lead me to it. He was helping me put the to help me learn my job. In the calling world, however, in the purpose world, in the allow God to be your CEO world, it is faith and work, it is endurance and discipline, it is diligence, it is grace and rest over grind and hustle, it is knowing when to be still so you know when to move, it is allowing yourself to be led and not walk in your own strength.

Knowing that I had to start walking in this new version of myself, I started to set up my atmosphere and environment. I started to get rid of everything that was not serving me anymore. My perspective started to change, I realized that my home had a lot of dark colors, blacks, and browns, and I no longer wanted anything that was dark in my home.

It was a real thing for me.

Black to me represented my depression, it represented the old version of me, it was something about it now that didn't sit right in my spirit. I looked around my home and everything seemed dark and gloomy. It never looked this way to me before but I thought about how I was transitioning in my life and how my mind was renewing so my perspective was also changing. I had prayed for a healthy perspective because I dealt with major depression for so long, so these colors represented the old version of me, it was time to set up my new atmosphere. I grabbed some trash bags and either donated or threw out what did not serve me in this new season. For me personally, I had to set up what a healthy environment meant to me so that I could allow joy, peace, and grace into my life so that I could fully flourish in this new space that I was entering. My desk was black I painted it white, and my walls had a lot of dark pictures up, I exchanged those for white frames with inspirational quotes, I started to see my home match what I was feeling on the inside and that was important to me.

As I set my atmosphere, two bible verses kept coming to me: Mark 4:27 and Galatians 6:9.

Mark 4:27 - He sleeps and rises night and day; the seed sprouts and grows, although he doesn't know how.

Galatians 6:9 - Let us not get tired of doing good, for we will reap at the proper time if we don't give up.

I realized that I needed to stand on these two bible verses as I prepared for the birth of Journey Written. I needed to stand on these as I maintained all of the work I have done because it was important that I continue to do the inner work to keep my inner healing muscles strong. Little did I know change was happening and I didn't really know what was going on but I started to feel shifts and transitions in my life happening.

Journal Entry 7.21 - "Hey God, it's me. There are a lot of things going on in my life. I can feel the shifts. Please don't leave me. I feel alone, please have your Holy Spirit comfort me. God I trust you."

On July 22nd, I had a dream. I had a dream that I was pregnant, and that I was in labor but it wasn't time to deliver the baby yet so they sent me back home. I woke up thinking: *what was that about?* As I journaled it came to me that the dream symbolized me birthing Journey Written and how I was about to get ready to launch. It was a reminder to not launch too early, but that I am in the contraction stage – finishing up some things and some loose ends and then I would know when it was time. As I closed up my journal, I thought to myself *what do mothers do to prepare to deliver their babies?* The first thing I thought about was they have a baby bag that is ready for when they go to the hospital.

I quickly opened up my bible to Luke 14:28: "For which of you, wanting to build a tower, doesn't first sit down and calculate the cost to see if he has enough to complete it." What was the cost of delivering Journey Written? What was my baby bag going to consist of?

I excitedly started to write:

- Faith
- Trust
- Tithing every week
- Intentional time with God every single day
- Peace and handing all my worries to God (Philippians 4:6-7)
- Authority and walking in the fullness of it every day
- Laughter

- Enjoying the journey
- Psalm 23:1
- Isaiah 41:10
- Mark 4:27
- Matthew 6:33-34
- Philippians 4:6-7
- Gratitude Daily
- Praise Daily
- The Armor of God (Ephesians 6:10-18)
- Ecclesiastes 5:18-20
- Patience, Endurance, & a Steadfast Spirit

This was the bag I needed to bring into the delivery room. I also felt my spirit lead me to write down the fruits of the spirit: love, joy, peace, patience, kindness, goodness, faithfulness, gentleness, and self-control (Galatians 5:22-23). It was important to list these out because anything opposite would be a reminder that I was working in the flesh, so I had to put my focus on praying for wisdom, understanding, and discernment to help me stay on the right path and decipher the two.

Whew, this was a lot.

I knew that it was going to require more work but not this much. This is what I needed to do to properly prepare for birth and then help this baby grow up.

THE BIRTH

I walked into August feeling good. It was my birthday month, we were still in the pilot program, and it was going really well. I got clarity that my launch was supposed to happen in September, even though I didn't get an exact date yet. My life was full of love from family, friends, and loved ones. I couldn't ask for a better time especially during a season where we all were still isolated and in quarantine.

One day I looked at my business bank account and instantly got sad. I still was struggling to pay my business expenses and get any profitability. I felt like I had been doing everything right but still couldn't get to a place that I wanted to be which was debt-free and making money. Slowly my mind tried to slip back into negative thinking. I started to get more and more anxious, and isolation and loneliness tried to creep in, but this was my time to fight back.

Brit you have been in this same situation plenty of times, you got this.

I had to remind myself that this was not a sprint but a marathon. I could tell my mind was trying to be distracted again by things seen, but I had to stay focused on things not seen yet.

As the time got closer to pushing Journey Written out, I started to get a bit fearful of success, of judgment, of what other people were going to say about me:

"Oh she always doing something....

All you do is be successful...

Dang what you doing next Brit...

Oh you don't want to settle down and have a family yet, have some fun...."

The list can go on and on.

I know what people have said under their breath and to my face so I could only imagine what people were going to say when I released a Book Writing and publishing Company. I started to become embarrassed of my successes because they were not what society was used to. I started to think I was weird. I started not wanting to birth Journey Written anymore because I didn't want to be seen as just being known as successful. I was more than that. Again, I started to drift into all of these thoughts, and judgments, and I started to feel rejected without even releasing anything. I felt like I was going through a serious emotional and mental rollercoaster, the closer and closer I got to the launch of Journey Written.

I was in Spiritual Warfare. My mind and flesh were trying to win, but I couldn't let them. I was prepared to fight.

I was still praying every day, being in my word, affirming over my life, and journaling. I fasted one day per week – fasting was something I started in early July and decided to dedicate myself to.

Everything that did not concern me or my bigger purpose had to go or get said "no" to.

I thought about the tools that I put in place, and it was time to use them. I had to put my FULL Armor on. I had to go back to my baby bag. I had to get back centered, I had to remember this was my contraction season. I went back to my journal flipping through my pages to find some inspiration, to find my baby bag that I wrote down.

I found it!

I read through my bible verses that told me to release all my cares to God (Philippians 4:6-7). I then journaled and left every last worry on that paper so that I can move forward in the fruit of the spirit of Peace.

It was then, I got confirmation that my launch was to be September 17th, 2020.

Mentally, emotionally, physically, financially, and spiritually I was tired.

I was exhausted.

I thought about the patience, endurance, & steadfast spirit I wrote down in my baby bag on 7/22. It was time to refill my spirit back up. I was too close to the finish line. One of my friends reminded me that birthing is not for the faint of heart: that birthing takes time, and contractions do not feel good. Birthing takes energy, and that I had to PUSH. I looked up endurance devotionals in the bible app and switched my mindset to I am training for birth. I started to get back up super early and work on my website, pushing through and working on my creativity.

Faith and works were in full action. I walked in the authority that God granted me.

On 9/17/20, Journey Written was released to the world. I finally did it. I pushed out this company that would help women release their testimony, that would help women publish their unique story.

What a journey it has been!

I didn't know that inner healing, wholeness, self-worth, and confidence all had something in common. It was like a ripple effect I had never seen before. It took me a while but I finally fully accepted that I was God's vessel in this company, that He trusted me to do this thing to help His women break free.

I am called to help women to wholeness through my books and workbooks and Journey Written is to help the ready women release their stories, these are the women who have done the inner healing work and are able to tell their story with authority. They just need help with pulling it fully out and guidance on structure, which is how God was using me. Who would have thought, all the work I did for my inner healing would help another woman? Who would have thought that the books that I personally wrote and all of the information that I posted or spoke on my podcast would lead to me truly finding out my gifts?

I thought that I was going to work in corporate forever and just rise to the top and be an executive one day, but God had other plans. He needed me to be His executive as He is the CEO. He needed me to do His work for the kingdom with excellence, confidence, and grace. Looking back this journey was a complete rollercoaster. I cried almost every day, I was isolated a lot, and I lost myself in the process, but birthed a new version of myself that I have fallen in love with. Everything has definitely worked together for the good. I am whole. I am happy. I am helping other women get to the place of wholeness and also helping them release their story because their story is worth living, it is worth telling.

It's so beautiful to me how BnPowered turned into Journey Written, and I didn't even realize it until later 2020. In BnPowered I always told people to BnPowered by their story, journey, and life. I told them that their story mattered, and if it was worth living then why not make it worth telling. It is so beautiful how God uses you, and uses everything for the good of those who love Him. I had the plan the whole time. He provided me my purpose long ago, I just needed to go through the lessons, through the healing, through the acceptance, to finally see it come into full fruition. I love God for being patient with me during this season. I love Him for granting me so much favor. This journey has definitely not been easy for me, but I had to trust each and every step. I had to grow my faith, and I had to believe and execute. I thank God for ordering each and every one of my steps, for being patient with me as I grew my relationship with Him in this season, I can't lie it has been the best relationship in my life and it has overflowed into my human relationships. I laugh more, I enjoy the gifts of life more, and most importantly I learned that my calling is bringing God's women to wholeness and teaching them how to release and write their stories. Throughout this whole journey I learned so many valuable lessons, so much character development happened as I have been going through these last three years and I know that this is only the beginning of what God has in store for me.

Your story is worth living and why not BnPowered to make it worth telling!

ENJOY
PICTURES OF THE JOURNEY

BEAUTIFULLY BROKEN T-SHIRT
First Shirt to Sell

WORKOUT SHIRTS & FITNESS JOURNAL
When I slowly drifted to fitness as a focus

ARMOR OF WORDS
Armor of Words Book Signing

THE PODCAST
Started January 2020

JOURNEY WRITTEN
The paper hanging up on my wall

Social Media Launch Day Post:

God we did it. I pray you are proud of me.

I want to introduce Journey Written my Book Writing & Publishing Company. I thought about getting professional pics and everything for the launch but I wanted to show you all my place where I birthed this busiess. While on this journey I had to remember "Pray about everything, worry about nothing."

Thank you God for ordering my steps, being the CEO, and trusting me to be your vessel. All the glory belogins to Him.

LAUNCH DAY: 9.17.20

JOURNEY WRITTEN CLIENT TESTIMONIAL

"I chose to work with Journey Written because I needed help writing my story of rejection. This was more than a book for me. This book is my testimony and a story of how I overcame my battle with the stronghold of rejection. I specifically chose to work with this company because Brit Lashae specializes in inner healing and that is what my book is about. I knew she would challenge me to write and share my story in a way that would be raw and relatable but also empower my readers to heal and do their inner healing work.

The Book Writing Coaching experience was amazing. I like how detailed and organized Brit Lashae was throughout my experience working with her. From the very first meeting, I knew I had made the right decision to work with Journey Written. The weekly Zoom sessions and accountability emails were my favorite part of the book writing coaching journey. I looked forward to the weekly check-ins and I appreciated the weekly accountability emails sent to me every Saturday. Those emails were my reminder and motivation to stay on track in my writing process.

The best part of working with Journey Written was the relationship I developed with the owner, Brit Lashae. She really inspired me and motivated me throughout the entire experience. She challenged me at times and really made me dig deep within myself to share parts of my story that I didn't think

I could. She also was extremely organized and time-oriented. She made my entire book-writing and self-publishing process easy. All I had to do was focus on the writing and she helped me with the rest.

My favorite part of the journey was when she helped me develop the self-coaching questions in my book. That was my biggest challenge in the writing process. Since inner healing is her expertise, she was able to help write and develop inner healing questions for each phase of my book and gave me weekly feedback on the questions I created. I appreciate that more than she knows!

I loved my experience working with Journey Written and I cannot wait to work with them again for my next book.

I would absolutely recommend other women to work with Journey Written. Writing a book is a journey within itself. Especially, a book you are writing about sharing a traumatic experience in your life. It takes a special person to help you go through that journey. Sharing your story can be triggering and Journey Written helps you overcome your triggers and focus on your why. Not all book coaches have the capability to do this.

Not only does Journey Written help you overcome your triggers, Journey Written helps you through every step of your book writing process. From the initial book outline to the final step of publishing your book through your selected self-publishing company, you don't have to worry about a thing!"

~ Amber B.

JOURNEY WRITTEN CLIENT TESTIMONIAL

"Working with Journey Written was a life-changing experience for me. Not only did I gain a book writing coach, but I also gained an accountability partner as well as someone who believed in the impact and the success of my book. The book writing process itself was challenging and there were days when I became extremely overwhelmed. I even let fear and doubt discourage me. But Brit was heaven sent. She was the most kind, patient, and encouraging coach that I have ever worked with. She gave me the courage I needed when I was too overwhelmed to believe in myself. If you are interested in telling your story and want to work with a company that is led by the holy-spirit then Journey Written is the company for you. Brit was straightforward and honest about any and every question that I asked her. But most of all she was supportive. One of the things I enjoyed the most about Journey Written was the weekly check-ins we would have. I got the opportunity to meet with her virtually every week to discuss the progress of my book. On top of that, she would check up on me during the week via email. She was always on top of things and she left no room for confusion or miscommunication. I definitely recommend working with Journey written."

~LaKrystal L.

I HAVE
 a healthy *balance* of work, play, & rest. I honor the person that I am.

MEET THE AUTHOR
BRIT LASHAE

Brit Lashae is an Author & Book-Writing Coach for women. She founded Journey Written in 2020 and has a passion for helping aspiring authors tell their story and testimony.

Other books by Brit Lashae:

Armor of Words

Triggered Book & Workbook

WORK WITH JOURNEY WRITTEN

Journey Written® is a Book-Writing & Publishing company for the Aspiring Author READY to leave her mark and write her story into a published book.

We would love to work with you to publish your unique story. Learn more about us at: **www.journeywritten.com**

Social: IG, Facebook, Twitter, LinkedIn: **@journeywritten**

ESTHER 4:14

"...Who knows, perhaps you have come to your royal position for *such a time as this*."

www.ingramcontent.com/pod-product-compliance
Lightning Source LLC
Chambersburg PA
CBHW070426080426
42450CB00030B/1501